This Travel Journal Belongs To:

AREA *Suggestions*

PLACES TO VISIT:

Logroño

San Millán de la Colloga

Briones

Santo Domingo de la Calzada

Alfaro

Trevijano

Haro

Laguardia

Calahorra

Arnedo

Nájera

Clavijo

Ezcaray

San Vincente de la Sonsierra

Sajazarra

Bilbão

LA RIOJA WINE REGIONS:

Rioja Alta

Rioja Baja

Rioja Alavesa

Greater Rioja

THINGS TO DO & SEE:

La Rioja Wine Tours

Hike the Camino de Santiago

Tierra Rapaz – Raptor Park

Monasterio de San Millán de Yuso

Monasterio de San Millán de Suso

Dinastía Vivanco – Museum of Wine

Parque del Espolón

Santo Domingo de la Calzada Cathedral

Museo Würth La Rioja – Modern Art

Church of San Bartolomé

Mirador de las Ciguenas

Museo de la Rioja

Canyon of Leza River

Monasterio de Santa María la Real

See the Architecture of Bodegas Ysios & Marques de Riscal

Wander Bodegas Muga

Ruins of the Monastario de San Prudencio

Bodegas del Marqués de Vargas

The Guggenheim Museum - Bilbão

LA RIOJA *Bucket List*

PLACES I WANT TO VISIT:

THINGS I WANT TO DO:

TOP 3 DESTINATIONS:

TRAVEL *Planner*

DESTINATION:	DATES:

BUDGET:	WEATHER:	CURRENCY EXCHANGE:

ACCOMODATION OVERVIEW

NAME:	LOCATION:	DATE:	ADDRESS:

NOTES & TRAVEL DETAILS

TRIP BUDGET *Planner*

TRIP DETAILS:

AMOUNT NEEDED:

OUR GOAL DATE:

DEPOSIT TRACKER

AMOUNT DEPOSITED: **DATE DEPOSITED:**

TRAVEL EXPENSE *Tracker*

DESTINATION: BUDGET GOAL:

DATE:	DESCRIPTION:	CURRENCY:	AMOUNT:

TOTAL EXPENSES:

TRAVEL EXPENSE *Tracker*

DESTINATION: _____   BUDGET GOAL: _____

DATE:	DESCRIPTION:	CURRENCY:	AMOUNT:

TOTAL EXPENSES:

FLIGHT *Information*

DATE: _____   DESTINATION: _____

AIRLINE:	
BOOKING NUMBER:	
DEPARTURE DATE:	
BOARDING TIME:	
GATE NUMBER	
SEAT NUMBER:	
FLIGHT DURATION:	
ARRIVAL / LANDING TIME:	

DATE: _____   DESTINATION: _____

AIRLINE:	
BOOKING NUMBER:	
DEPARTURE DATE:	
BOARDING TIME:	
GATE NUMBER	
SEAT NUMBER:	
FLIGHT DURATION:	
ARRIVAL / LANDING TIME:	

TRAIN *Information*

DATE: _____ DESTINATION: _____

TRAIN PASS (EURAIL, ETC.):	
DEPARTING STATION:	
DEPARTURE DATE:	
BOARDING TIME:	
GATE NUMBER:	
SEAT NUMBER:	
ARRIVAL STATION:	
ARRIVAL / LANDING TIME:	

DATE: _____ DESTINATION: _____

TRAIN PASS (EURAIL, ETC.):	
DEPARTING STATION:	
DEPARTURE DATE:	
BOARDING TIME:	
GATE NUMBER:	
SEAT NUMBER:	
ARRIVAL STATION:	
ARRIVAL / LANDING TIME:	

TRAIN *Information*

DATE: _____   DESTINATION: _____

TRAIN PASS (EURAIL, ETC.):	
DEPARTING STATION:	
DEPARTURE DATE:	
BOARDING TIME:	
GATE NUMBER:	
SEAT NUMBER:	
ARRIVAL STATION:	
ARRIVAL / LANDING TIME:	

DATE: _____   DESTINATION: _____

TRAIN PASS (EURAIL, ETC.):	
DEPARTING STATION:	
DEPARTURE DATE:	
BOARDING TIME:	
GATE NUMBER:	
SEAT NUMBER:	
ARRIVAL STATION:	
ARRIVAL / LANDING TIME:	

VEHICLE *Information*

TYPE: PERSONAL RENTAL

CAR RENTAL AGENCY:	
CONTACT INFORMATION:	
PICK UP DATE AND TIME:	
RETURN DATE AND TIME:	
MAKE & MODEL:	
INSPECTION NOTES:	
COST PER DAY:	
TOTAL COST:	

TYPE: GUIDED TOUR RENTAL

TOUR BUS RENTAL:	
TOUR COMPANY CONTACT:	
TOUR GUIDE NAME:	
DEPARTURE DATE AND TIME:	
LOCATIONS TO BE VISITED:	
COST PER TICKET:	
TOTAL COST FOR GROUP:	

TRAVEL *Planner*

PRE-TRAVEL CHECKLIST

1 MONTH BEFORE	2 WEEKS BEFORE
☐	☐
☐	☐
☐	☐
☐	☐
☐	☐

1 WEEK BEFORE	2 DAYS BEFORE
☐	☐
☐	☐
☐	☐
☐	☐
☐	☐

24 HOURS BEFORE	DAY OF TRAVEL
☐	☐
☐	☐
☐	☐
☐	☐
☐	☐

TRIP TO DO *List*

☐

☐

☐

☐

☐

☐

☐

☐

☐

PACKING *Check List*

DOCUMENTS

- [ ] PASSPORT
- [ ] DRIVER'S LICENSE
- [ ] VISA
- [ ] PLANE TICKETS
- [ ] LOCAL CURRENCY
- [ ] INSURANCE CARD
- [ ] HEALTH CARD
- [ ] OTHER ID
- [ ] HOTEL INFO
- [ ] _____

CLOTHING

- [ ] SOCKS
- [ ] SWIM WEAR
- [ ] T-SHIRTS
- [ ] JEANS/PANTS
- [ ] SHORTS
- [ ] SKIRTS / DRESSES
- [ ] JACKET / COAT
- [ ] SLEEPWEAR
- [ ] SHOES
- [ ] _____

PERSONAL ITEMS

- [ ] SHAMPOO
- [ ] RAZORS
- [ ] COSMETICS
- [ ] HAIR BRUSH
- [ ] LIP BALM
- [ ] WATER BOTTLE
- [ ] SOAP
- [ ] TOOTHBRUSH
- [ ] JEWELRY
- [ ] _____

ELECTRONICS

- [ ] CELL PHONE
- [ ] CHARGER
- [ ] LAPTOP
- [ ] BATTERIES
- [ ] EARPHONES
- [ ] CAMERA
- [ ] MEMORY CARD
- [ ] _____
- [ ] _____
- [ ] _____

HEALTH & SAFETY

- [ ] HAND SANITIZER
- [ ] SUNSCREEN
- [ ] VITAMIN
- [ ] BANDAIDS
- [ ] ADVIL/TYLENOL
- [ ] GLASSES
- [ ] COLD/FLU MEDS
- [ ] _____
- [ ] _____
- [ ] _____

ESSENTIALS

- [ ] _____
- [ ] _____
- [ ] _____
- [ ] _____
- [ ] _____
- [ ] _____
- [ ] _____
- [ ] _____
- [ ] _____
- [ ] _____

PACKING *Check List*

DATE OF TRIP: **DURATION:**

OUTFIT *Planner*

DAY: DESTINATION: PACKED: ☐

DAY: EVENING:

ACTIVITY:

OUTFIT:

SHOES:

ACC:

DAY: DESTINATION: PACKED: ☐

DAY: EVENING:

ACTIVITY:

OUTFIT:

SHOES:

ACC:

DAY: DESTINATION: PACKED: ☐

DAY: EVENING:

ACTIVITY:

OUTFIT:

SHOES:

ACC:

OUTFIT *Planner*

DAY: DESTINATION: PACKED: ☐

DAY: EVENING:

ACTIVITY:

OUTFIT:

SHOES:

ACC:

DAY: DESTINATION: PACKED: ☐

DAY: EVENING:

ACTIVITY:

OUTFIT:

SHOES:

ACC:

DAY: DESTINATION: PACKED: ☐

DAY: EVENING:

ACTIVITY:

OUTFIT:

SHOES:

ACC:

OUTFIT *Planner*

DAY: DESTINATION: PACKED: ☐

DAY:

EVENING:

ACTIVITY:

OUTFIT:

SHOES:

ACC:

DAY: DESTINATION: PACKED: ☐

DAY:

EVENING:

ACTIVITY:

OUTFIT:

SHOES:

ACC:

DAY: DESTINATION: PACKED: ☐

DAY:

EVENING:

ACTIVITY:

OUTFIT:

SHOES:

ACC:

OUTFIT *Planner*

DAY: DESTINATION: PACKED: ☐

DAY: EVENING:

ACTIVITY:

OUTFIT:

SHOES:

ACC:

DAY: DESTINATION: PACKED: ☐

DAY: EVENING:

ACTIVITY:

OUTFIT:

SHOES:

ACC:

DAY: DESTINATION: PACKED: ☐

DAY: EVENING:

ACTIVITY:

OUTFIT:

SHOES:

ACC:

OUTFIT *Planner*

DAY: DESTINATION: PACKED: ☐

DAY:

EVENING:

ACTIVITY:

OUTFIT:

SHOES:

ACC:

DAY: DESTINATION: PACKED: ☐

DAY:

EVENING:

ACTIVITY:

OUTFIT:

SHOES:

ACC:

DAY: DESTINATION: PACKED: ☐

DAY:

EVENING:

ACTIVITY:

OUTFIT:

SHOES:

ACC:

OUTFIT *Planner*

DAY: DESTINATION: PACKED: ☐

           DAY: EVENING:

ACTIVITY:

OUTFIT:

SHOES:

ACC:

DAY: DESTINATION: PACKED: ☐

           DAY: EVENING:

ACTIVITY:

OUTFIT:

SHOES:

ACC:

DAY: DESTINATION: PACKED: ☐

           DAY: EVENING:

ACTIVITY:

OUTFIT:

SHOES:

ACC:

OUTFIT *Planner*

DAY:	DESTINATION:	PACKED: ☐

DAY:	EVENING:
ACTIVITY:	
OUTFIT:	
SHOES:	
ACC:	

DAY:	DESTINATION:	PACKED: ☐

DAY:	EVENING:
ACTIVITY:	
OUTFIT:	
SHOES:	
ACC:	

DAY:	DESTINATION:	PACKED: ☐

DAY:	EVENING:
ACTIVITY:	
OUTFIT:	
SHOES:	
ACC:	

OUTFIT *Planner*

DAY: DESTINATION: PACKED: ☐

DAY: EVENING:

ACTIVITY:

OUTFIT:

SHOES:

ACC:

DAY: DESTINATION: PACKED: ☐

DAY: EVENING:

ACTIVITY:

OUTFIT:

SHOES:

ACC:

DAY: DESTINATION: PACKED: ☐

DAY: EVENING:

ACTIVITY:

OUTFIT:

SHOES:

ACC:

TRAVEL *Checklist*

DESTINATION: RIOJA ALTA   DATES:

NOTABLE TOWNS

Haro

Logroño

Nájera

San Vincente de la Sonsierra

Briñas

Brionas

THINGS TO SEE

The Church of San Bartolomé

Cathedral of Santa Maria de la Redonda

Hike the Camino de Santiago

Castillo de San Vincente

POPULAR HOTELS

Hotel Pura Vida, Valgañón

Hotel Calle Mayor

POPULAR WINERIES

Bodegas Gómez Cruzado

Dinastía Vivanco – Museum of Wine

Bodegas La Rioja Alta S.A.

Bodegas Martinez Lacuesta La Rioja

Bodega Marqués de Murrieta

Bodegas Miguel Merino

Bodegas Conde de los Andes

Bodegas Muga

Bodegas Campo Viejo

 **Travel Tip:
Many wineries will
require reservations**

WHERE TO EAT

El Rincón del Noble

Restaurante Ariño

Restaurantes Rioja La Cueva de Doña Isabela

HOTEL *Information*

NAME OF HOTEL:

ADDRESS:

PHONE NUMBER:

CONFIRMATION #:

CHECK IN/OUT:

ROOM TYPE:

RATE:

NAME OF HOTEL:

ADDRESS:

PHONE NUMBER:

CONFIRMATION #:

CHECK IN/OUT:

ROOM TYPE:

RATE:

NOTES

TRAVEL *Itinerary*

DESTINATION: DATE:

MON

TUE

WED

THU

FRI

SAT

SUN

VACATION *Planner*

DAILY ITINERARY

DATE: _____

LOCATION: _____

BUDGET: _____

☀ ⛅ 🌧 ☁ ⛈

TOP ACTIVITIES

MEAL PLANNER

TIME:	SCHEDULE:

EXPENSES

TOTAL COST: _____

NOTES:

TRAVEL *Planner*

DATE:

DAY:

☀ ⛅ 🌦 ☁ ⛈

NOTES

6

7

8

9

10

11

12

1

REMINDERS

2

3

4

5

6

7

8

9

10

11

12

VACATION *Planner*

DAILY ITINERARY

DATE: _____

LOCATION: _____

BUDGET: _____

☀ ⛅ 🌦 ☁ ⛈

TOP ACTIVITIES

MEAL PLANNER

TIME: SCHEDULE:

EXPENSES

TOTAL COST:

NOTES:

TRAVEL *Planner*

DATE:

DAY:

NOTES

6

7

8

9

10

11

12

1

2

3

4

5

6

7

8

9

10

11

12

REMINDERS

TRAVEL *Notes*

DATE: LOCATION:

DATE: LOCATION:

TRAVEL *Journal*

DATE: _____

TRAVEL *Journal*

DATE: _____

WINE TASTING *Notes*

DATE: TOWN:

WINE NAME: **WINERY:**

TYPE OF GRAPE: **VINTAGE:**

APPEARANCE & SMELL:

TASTING NOTES: FLORAL   CITRUS   WOODSY   SPICE

PAIRING SUGGESTIONS:

FINAL RATING: ☆ ☆ ☆ ☆ ☆

TODAY'S FAVORITE MEMORIES:

WINE TASTING *Notes*

WINE NAME: **WINERY:**

TYPE OF GRAPE: **VINTAGE:**

APPEARANCE & SMELL:

TASTING NOTES: FLORAL   CITRUS   WOODSY   SPICE

PAIRING SUGGESTIONS:

FINAL RATING: ☆ ☆ ☆ ☆ ☆

TODAY'S FAVORITE MEMORIES:

WINE TASTING *Notes*

DATE: **TOWN:**

WINE NAME: **WINERY:**

TYPE OF GRAPE: **VINTAGE:**

APPEARANCE & SMELL:

TASTING NOTES: FLORAL   CITRUS   WOODSY   SPICE

PAIRING SUGGESTIONS:

FINAL RATING: ☆ ☆ ☆ ☆ ☆

TODAY'S FAVORITE MEMORIES:

WINE TASTING *Notes*

DATE: TOWN:

WINE NAME: **WINERY:**

TYPE OF GRAPE: **VINTAGE:**

APPEARANCE & SMELL:

TASTING NOTES: **FLORAL   CITRUS   WOODSY   SPICE**

PAIRING SUGGESTIONS:

FINAL RATING: ☆ ☆ ☆ ☆ ☆

TODAY'S FAVORITE MEMORIES:

TRAVEL *Journal*

DATE: _____

_____

_____

_____

_____

_____

_____

_____

_____

_____

_____

_____

_____

_____

_____

TRAVEL *Journal*

DATE: _____

_____

_____

_____

_____

_____

_____

_____

_____

_____

_____

_____

_____

_____

_____

_____

_____

_____

BEER TASTING *Notes*

DATE: TOWN:

BEER NAME: **BREWERY:**

TYPE OF HOPS: **TYPE OF BEER:**

APPEARANCE & BODY:

TASTING NOTES: HOPPY WOODSY CITRUS SOUR MALTY BITTER

PAIRING SUGGESTIONS:

FINAL RATING: ☆ ☆ ☆ ☆ ☆

TODAY'S FAVORITE MEMORIES:

BEER TASTING *Notes*

DATE: TOWN:

BEER NAME: **BREWERY:**

TYPE OF HOPS: **TYPE OF BEER:**

APPEARANCE & BODY:

TASTING NOTES: BITTER   HOPPY   CITRUS   SOUR   MALTY   FLORAL

PAIRING SUGGESTIONS:

FINAL RATING: ☆ ☆ ☆ ☆ ☆

TODAY'S FAVORITE MEMORIES:

TRAVEL *Journal*

DATE: _____

TRAVEL *Journal*

DATE: _____

_____

_____

_____

_____

_____

_____

_____

_____

_____

_____

_____

_____

_____

_____

_____

TRAVEL *Checklist*

DESTINATION: GREATER RIOJA   DATES:

NOTABLE TOWNS

San Millán de la Colloga

Santo Domingo de la Calzada

Ezcaray

Torrecilla en Cameros

Enciso

POPULAR WINERIES

BODEGAS FINCA LA EMPERATRIZ

Bodegas David Moreno La Rioja Alta

Bodegas Vinícola Real

POPULAR HOTELS

Echaurren Hotel Gastronomico

La Facultad de Castroviejo

THINGS TO DO

Winery Tours

Parque Natural Sierra de Cebollera

Las Pozas de Arnedillo

Monasterio de San Millán de Yuso

Monasterio de San Millán de Suso

Catedral de Santo Domingo de la Calzada

Hike the Camino de Santiago

Laguna Negra de Urbión

Find Dinosaur Footprints in Enciso

REGION GRAPES:
Temperanillo, Mazuelo, Graciano, & Garnacha

WHERE TO EAT

La Cueva del Chato

Los Acebos

Venta Moncalvillo

HOTEL *Information*

NAME OF HOTEL:

ADDRESS:

PHONE NUMBER:

CONFIRMATION #:

CHECK IN/OUT:

ROOM TYPE:

RATE:

NAME OF HOTEL:

ADDRESS:

PHONE NUMBER:

CONFIRMATION #:

CHECK IN/OUT:

ROOM TYPE:

RATE:

NOTES

TRAVEL *Itinerary*

DESTINATION: DATE:

MON

TUE

WED

THU

FRI

SAT

SUN

VACATION *Planner*

DAILY ITINERARY

DATE: _____

LOCATION: _____

BUDGET: _____

TOP ACTIVITIES

MEAL PLANNER

TIME: SCHEDULE:

EXPENSES

TOTAL COST: _____

NOTES:

TRAVEL *Planner*

NOTES

6

7

8

9

10

11

12

1

2

3

4

5

6

7

8

9

10

11

12

REMINDERS

VACATION *Planner*

DAILY ITINERARY

DATE:

LOCATION:

BUDGET:

TOP ACTIVITIES

MEAL PLANNER

TIME:

SCHEDULE:

EXPENSES

TOTAL COST:

NOTES:

TRAVEL *Planner*

DATE:

DAY:

NOTES

REMINDERS

6

7

8

9

10

11

12

1

2

3

4

5

6

7

8

9

10

11

12

TRAVEL *Notes*

DATE: LOCATION:

DATE: LOCATION:

WINE TASTING *Notes*

DATE: TOWN:

WINE NAME: **WINERY:**

TYPE OF GRAPE: **VINTAGE:**

APPEARANCE & SMELL:

TASTING NOTES: FLORAL   CITRUS   WOODSY   SPICY

PAIRING SUGGESTIONS:

FINAL RATING: ☆ ☆ ☆ ☆ ☆

TODAY'S FAVORITE MEMORIES:

WINE TASTING *Notes*

DATE:

TOWN:

WINE NAME:

WINERY:

TYPE OF GRAPE:

VINTAGE:

APPEARANCE & SMELL:

TASTING NOTES: **FLORAL**   **CITRUS**   **WOODSY**   **SPICE**

PAIRING SUGGESTIONS:

FINAL RATING: ☆ ☆ ☆ ☆ ☆

TODAY'S FAVORITE MEMORIES:

WINE TASTING *Notes*

WINE NAME: WINERY:

TYPE OF GRAPE: VINTAGE:

APPEARANCE & SMELL:

TASTING NOTES: FLORAL   CITRUS   WOODSY   SPICE

PAIRING SUGGESTIONS:

FINAL RATING: ☆ ☆ ☆ ☆ ☆

TODAY'S FAVORITE MEMORIES:

WINE TASTING *Notes*

DATE: TOWN:

WINE NAME: **WINERY:**

TYPE OF GRAPE: **VINTAGE:**

APPEARANCE & SMELL:

TASTING NOTES: FLORAL   CITRUS   WOODSY   SPICE

PAIRING SUGGESTIONS:

FINAL RATING: ☆ ☆ ☆ ☆ ☆

TODAY'S FAVORITE MEMORIES:

TRAVEL *Journal*

DATE: _____

TRAVEL *Journal*

DATE: _____

_____

_____

_____

_____

_____

_____

_____

_____

_____

_____

_____

_____

_____

_____

_____

_____

_____

TRAVEL *Journal*

DATE: _____

WINE TASTING *Notes*

DATE:

DATE: TOWN:

WINE NAME: WINERY:

TYPE OF GRAPE: VINTAGE:

APPEARANCE & SMELL:

TASTING NOTES: FLORAL   CITRUS   WOODSY   SPICE

PAIRING SUGGESTIONS:

FINAL RATING: ☆ ☆ ☆ ☆ ☆

TODAY'S FAVORITE MEMORIES:

WINE TASTING *Notes*

DATE: TOWN:

WINE NAME: **WINERY:**

TYPE OF GRAPE: **VINTAGE:**

APPEARANCE & SMELL:

TASTING NOTES: **FLORAL   CITRUS   WOODSY   SPICE**

PAIRING SUGGESTIONS:

FINAL RATING: ☆ ☆ ☆ ☆ ☆

TODAY'S FAVORITE MEMORIES:

TRAVEL *Journal*

DATE: _____

TRAVEL *Journal*

DATE: _____

TRAVEL *Checklist*

DESTINATION: RIOJA BAJA   **DATES:**

NOTABLE TOWNS

Alfaro

Arnedo

Calahorra

Clavijo

POPULAR WINERIES

Bodega Viña Real

Viñedos del Contino

Bodega Marques De Montecierzo Upeltegia

Bodegas Corral (Don James)

AREA HOTELS

Finca de los Arandinos

THINGS TO DO

Winery Tours

Tierra Rapaz – Raptor Park

Catedral de Calahorra

Colegiata de San Miguel Arcángel & Mirador de las Cigüeñas

Monasterio de San José

Cuevas de los Cien Pilares & Cuevas de Los Palomares

Castillo de Arnedo

Monasterio de Nuestra Señora de Vico

Castillo de Clavijo

REGION GRAPES:
Garnacha

WHERE TO EAT

Maher

Bodega Pago de Cirsus

Restaurante Coliceo 29

HOTEL *Information*

NAME OF HOTEL:

ADDRESS:

PHONE NUMBER:

CONFIRMATION #:

CHECK IN/OUT:

ROOM TYPE:

RATE:

NAME OF HOTEL:

ADDRESS:

PHONE NUMBER:

CONFIRMATION #:

CHECK IN/OUT:

ROOM TYPE:

RATE:

NOTES

TRAVEL *Itinerary*

DESTINATION: DATE:

MON

TUE

WED

THU

FRI

SAT

SUN

VACATION *Planner*

DAILY ITINERARY

DATE: _____

LOCATION: _____

BUDGET: _____

TOP ACTIVITIES

MEAL PLANNER

EXPENSES

TIME: SCHEDULE:

TOTAL COST:

NOTES:

TRAVEL *Planner*

DATE: _____

DAY: _____

☀ ⛅ 🌦 ☁ ⛈

6 _____

7 _____

8 _____

9 _____

10 _____

11 _____

12 _____

1 _____

2 _____

3 _____

4 _____

5 _____

6 _____

7 _____

8 _____

9 _____

10 _____

11 _____

12 _____

NOTES

REMINDERS

TRAVEL *Planner*

DATE: DAY:

NOTES

6

7

8

9

10

11

REMINDERS

12

1

2

3

4

5

6

7

8

9

10

11

12

TRAVEL *Notes*

DATE: LOCATION:

DATE: LOCATION:

WINE TASTING *Notes*

DATE: TOWN:

WINE NAME: **WINERY:**

TYPE OF GRAPE: **VINTAGE:**

APPEARANCE & SMELL:

TASTING NOTES: FLORAL   CITRUS   WOODSY   SPICE

PAIRING SUGGESTIONS:

FINAL RATING: ☆ ☆ ☆ ☆ ☆

TODAY'S FAVORITE MEMORIES:

WINE TASTING *Notes*

DATE: **TOWN:**

WINE NAME: **WINERY:**

TYPE OF GRAPE: **VINTAGE:**

APPEARANCE & SMELL:

TASTING NOTES: FLORAL   CITRUS   WOODSY   SPICE

PAIRING SUGGESTIONS:

FINAL RATING: ☆ ☆ ☆ ☆ ☆

TODAY'S FAVORITE MEMORIES:

WINE TASTING *Notes*

DATE: TOWN:

WINE NAME: **WINERY:**

TYPE OF GRAPE: **VINTAGE:**

APPEARANCE & SMELL:

TASTING NOTES: FLORAL   CITRUS   WOODSY   SPICE

PAIRING SUGGESTIONS:

FINAL RATING: ☆ ☆ ☆ ☆ ☆

TODAY'S FAVORITE MEMORIES:

WINE TASTING *Notes*

WINE NAME: **WINERY:**

TYPE OF GRAPE: **VINTAGE:**

APPEARANCE & SMELL:

TASTING NOTES: FLORAL   CITRUS   WOODSY   SPICE

PAIRING SUGGESTIONS:

FINAL RATING: ☆ ☆ ☆ ☆ ☆

TODAY'S FAVORITE MEMORIES:

TRAVEL *Journal*

DATE: _____

WINE TASTING *Notes*

DATE:

TOWN:

WINE NAME:

WINERY:

TYPE OF GRAPE:

VINTAGE:

APPEARANCE & SMELL:

TASTING NOTES: **FLORAL   CITRUS   WOODSY   SPICE**

PAIRING SUGGESTIONS:

FINAL RATING: ☆ ☆ ☆ ☆ ☆

TODAY'S FAVORITE MEMORIES:

WINE TASTING *Notes*

DATE: TOWN:

WINE NAME: **WINERY:**

TYPE OF GRAPE: **VINTAGE:**

APPEARANCE & SMELL:

TASTING NOTES: **FLORAL**   **CITRUS**   **WOODSY**   **SPICE**

PAIRING SUGGESTIONS:

FINAL RATING: ☆ ☆ ☆ ☆ ☆

TODAY'S FAVORITE MEMORIES:

TRAVEL *Journal*

DATE: _____

_____

_____

_____

_____

_____

_____

_____

_____

_____

_____

_____

_____

_____

TRAVEL *Journal*

DATE: _____

TRAVEL *Journal*

DATE: _____

_____

_____

_____

_____

_____

_____

_____

_____

_____

_____

_____

_____

TRAVEL *Journal*

DATE: _____

Let's TRAVEL THE World

TRAVEL *Journal*

DATE: _____

TRAVEL *Checklist*

DESTINATION: RIOJA ALAVESA   DATES:

NOTABLE TOWNS

Laguardia

Elciego

Samaniego

Páganos

Eskuernaga

POPULAR WINERIES

Bodegas Luis Cañas

Bodega Finca Valpiedra

Bodegas Tritium S.

Bodegas Fernández de Piérola, S.L.

POPULAR HOTELS

Hotel Viura

Hospederia de los Parajes

THINGS TO DO

Winery Tours

See the Architecture of Bodegas Ysios

Hike Sierra de Cantabria

Church of Santa María de los Reyes

Tour Bodegas Campillo

Vinedos y Bodegas de la Marquesa

Take a Hot Air Balloon Ride

Excursion to the Guggenheim Museum in Bilbao

Kayak the River Ebro

**Regional Wines:
Temperanillo**

WHERE TO EAT

Bodegas Restaurante Luis Alegre

Eguren Ugarte

Villa Lucía Espacio Gastronómico

HOTEL *Information*

NAME OF HOTEL:

ADDRESS:

PHONE NUMBER:

CONFIRMATION #:

CHECK IN/OUT:

ROOM TYPE:

RATE:

NAME OF HOTEL:

ADDRESS:

PHONE NUMBER:

CONFIRMATION #:

CHECK IN/OUT:

ROOM TYPE:

RATE:

NOTES

TRAVEL *Itinerary*

DESTINATION: DATE:

MON

TUE

WED

THU

FRI

SAT

SUN

VACATION *Planner*

DAILY ITINERARY

DATE: _____

LOCATION: _____

BUDGET: _____

TOP ACTIVITIES

MEAL PLANNER

TIME: SCHEDULE:

EXPENSES

TOTAL COST: _____

NOTES:

TRAVEL *Planner*

DATE: DAY:

NOTES

☀ ⛅ 🌦 ☁ ⛈

6

7

8

9

10

11   REMINDERS

12

1

2

3

4

5

6

7

8

9

10

11

12

TRAVEL *Planner*

DATE:

DAY:

NOTES

REMINDERS

6

7

8

9

10

11

12

1

2

3

4

5

6

7

8

9

10

11

12

TRAVEL *Notes*

DATE: LOCATION:

DATE: LOCATION:

WINE TASTING *Notes*

DATE: TOWN:

WINE NAME: **WINERY:**

TYPE OF GRAPE: **VINTAGE:**

APPEARANCE & SMELL:

TASTING NOTES: **FLORAL**   **CITRUS**   **WOODSY**   **SPICE**

PAIRING SUGGESTIONS:

FINAL RATING: ☆ ☆ ☆ ☆ ☆

TODAY'S FAVORITE MEMORIES:

WINE TASTING *Notes*

DATE: TOWN:

WINE NAME: **WINERY:**

TYPE OF GRAPE: **VINTAGE:**

APPEARANCE & SMELL:

TASTING NOTES: **FLORAL   CITRUS   WOODSY   SPICE**

PAIRING SUGGESTIONS:

FINAL RATING: ☆ ☆ ☆ ☆ ☆

TODAY'S FAVORITE MEMORIES:

WINE TASTING *Notes*

DATE: TOWN:

WINE NAME: **WINERY:**

TYPE OF GRAPE: **VINTAGE:**

APPEARANCE & SMELL:

TASTING NOTES: FLORAL   CITRUS   WOODSY   SPICE

PAIRING SUGGESTIONS:

FINAL RATING: ☆ ☆ ☆ ☆ ☆

TODAY'S FAVORITE MEMORIES:

WINE TASTING *Notes*

DATE: TOWN:

WINE NAME: **WINERY:**

TYPE OF GRAPE: **VINTAGE:**

APPEARANCE & SMELL:

TASTING NOTES: **FLORAL**   **CITRUS**   **WOODSY**   **SPICE**

PAIRING SUGGESTIONS:

FINAL RATING: ☆ ☆ ☆ ☆ ☆

TODAY'S FAVORITE MEMORIES:

WINE TASTING *Notes*

DATE: TOWN:

WINE NAME: **WINERY:**

TYPE OF GRAPE: **VINTAGE:**

APPEARANCE & SMELL:

TASTING NOTES: FLORAL   CITRUS   WOODSY   SPICE

PAIRING SUGGESTIONS:

FINAL RATING: ☆ ☆ ☆ ☆ ☆

TODAY'S FAVORITE MEMORIES:

WINE TASTING *Notes*

DATE: TOWN:

WINE NAME: **WINERY:**

TYPE OF GRAPE: **VINTAGE:**

APPEARANCE & SMELL:

TASTING NOTES: FLORAL   CITRUS   WOODSY   SPICE

PAIRING SUGGESTIONS:

FINAL RATING: ☆ ☆ ☆ ☆ ☆

TODAY'S FAVORITE MEMORIES:

TRAVEL *Journal*

DATE: _____

TRAVEL *Journal*

DATE: _____

TRAVEL *Journal*

DATE: _____

_____

_____

_____

_____

_____

_____

_____

_____

_____

_____

_____

_____

_____

_____

_____

TRAVEL *Checklist*

DESTINATION: | DATES:

POPULAR HOTELS

THINGS TO DO

POPULAR WINERIES

WHERE TO EAT & DRINK

RECOMMENDATIONS

VACATION *Planner*

DAILY ITINERARY

DATE:

LOCATION:

BUDGET:

TOP ACTIVITIES

MEAL PLANNER

TIME:

SCHEDULE:

EXPENSES

TOTAL COST:

NOTES:

TRAVEL *Planner*

NOTES

6

7

8

9

10

11

12

1

2

3

REMINDERS

4

5

6

7

8

9

10

11

12

TRAVEL *Journal*

DATE: _____

WINE TASTING *Notes*

DATE: TOWN:

WINE NAME: **WINERY:**

TYPE OF GRAPE: **VINTAGE:**

APPEARANCE & SMELL:

TASTING NOTES: FLORAL   CITRUS   WOODSY   SPICE

PAIRING SUGGESTIONS:

FINAL RATING: ☆ ☆ ☆ ☆ ☆

TODAY'S FAVORITE MEMORIES:

WINE TASTING *Notes*

DATE: TOWN:

WINE NAME: **WINERY:**

TYPE OF GRAPE: **VINTAGE:**

APPEARANCE & SMELL:

TASTING NOTES: FLORAL   CITRUS   WOODSY   SPICE

PAIRING SUGGESTIONS:

FINAL RATING: ☆ ☆ ☆ ☆ ☆

TODAY'S FAVORITE MEMORIES:

WINE TASTING *Notes*

DATE: TOWN:

WINE NAME: **WINERY:**

TYPE OF GRAPE: **VINTAGE:**

APPEARANCE & SMELL:

TASTING NOTES: **FLORAL   CITRUS   WOODSY   SPICE**

PAIRING SUGGESTIONS:

FINAL RATING: ☆ ☆ ☆ ☆ ☆

TODAY'S FAVORITE MEMORIES:

WINE TASTING *Notes*

DATE: TOWN:

WINE NAME: **WINERY:**

TYPE OF GRAPE: **VINTAGE:**

APPEARANCE & SMELL:

TASTING NOTES: **FLORAL**   **CITRUS**   **WOODSY**   **SPICE**

PAIRING SUGGESTIONS:

FINAL RATING: ☆ ☆ ☆ ☆ ☆

TODAY'S FAVORITE MEMORIES:

TRAVEL *Journal*

_____

_____

_____

_____

_____

_____

_____

_____

_____

_____

_____

_____

_____

TRAVEL *Journal*

DATE: _____

_____

_____

_____

_____

_____

_____

_____

_____

_____

_____

_____

_____

TRAVEL *Checklist*

DESTINATION: DATES:

POPULAR HOTELS

THINGS TO DO

POPULAR WINERIES

RECOMMENDATIONS

WHERE TO EAT & DRINK

HOTEL *Information*

NAME OF HOTEL:

ADDRESS:

PHONE NUMBER:

CONFIRMATION #:

CHECK IN/OUT:

ROOM TYPE:

RATE:

NAME OF HOTEL:

ADDRESS:

PHONE NUMBER:

CONFIRMATION #:

CHECK IN/OUT:

ROOM TYPE:

RATE:

NOTES

TRAVEL *Itinerary*

DESTINATION: _____   DATE: _____

MON

TUE

WED

THU

FRI

SAT

SUN

VACATION *Planner*

DAILY ITINERARY

DATE: _____

LOCATION: _____

BUDGET: _____

TOP ACTIVITIES

MEAL PLANNER

TIME:	SCHEDULE:

EXPENSES

_____ _____

_____ _____

_____ _____

_____ _____

TOTAL COST: _____

NOTES:

TRAVEL *Planner*

DATE: _____   DAY: _____

NOTES

☀ ⛅ 🌦 ☁ ⛈

6

7

8

9

10

11   REMINDERS

12

1

2

3

4

5

6

7

8

9

10

11

12

TRAVEL *Planner*

DATE:

DAY:

☀️ 🌤️ 🌧️ ☁️ ⛈️

6

7

8

9

10

11

12

1

2

3

4

5

6

7

8

9

10

11

12

NOTES

REMINDERS

TRAVEL *Notes*

DATE: LOCATION:

DATE: LOCATION:

WINE TASTING *Notes*

DATE: TOWN:

WINE NAME: **WINERY:**

TYPE OF GRAPE: **VINTAGE:**

APPEARANCE & SMELL:

TASTING NOTES: FLORAL   CITRUS   WOODSY   SPICE

PAIRING SUGGESTIONS:

FINAL RATING: ☆ ☆ ☆ ☆ ☆

TODAY'S FAVORITE MEMORIES:

WINE TASTING *Notes*

DATE: TOWN:

WINE NAME: **WINERY:**

TYPE OF GRAPE: **VINTAGE:**

APPEARANCE & SMELL:

TASTING NOTES: **FLORAL**   **CITRUS**   **WOODSY**   **SPICE**

PAIRING SUGGESTIONS:

FINAL RATING: ☆ ☆ ☆ ☆ ☆

TODAY'S FAVORITE MEMORIES:

WINE TASTING *Notes*

DATE: TOWN:

WINE NAME: **WINERY:**

TYPE OF GRAPE: **VINTAGE:**

APPEARANCE & SMELL:

TASTING NOTES: FLORAL   CITRUS   WOODSY   SPICE

PAIRING SUGGESTIONS:

FINAL RATING: ☆ ☆ ☆ ☆ ☆

TODAY'S FAVORITE MEMORIES:

WINE TASTING *Notes*

DATE: TOWN:

WINE NAME: **WINERY:**

TYPE OF GRAPE: **VINTAGE:**

APPEARANCE & SMELL:

TASTING NOTES: **FLORAL**   **CITRUS**   **WOODSY**   **SPICE**

PAIRING SUGGESTIONS:

FINAL RATING: ☆ ☆ ☆ ☆ ☆

TODAY'S FAVORITE MEMORIES:

TRAVEL *Journal*

DATE: _____

TRAVEL *Journal*

DATE: _____

TRAVEL *Journal*

DATE: _____

_____

_____

_____

_____

_____

_____

_____

_____

_____

_____

_____

_____

_____

_____

_____

_____

_____

_____

TRAVEL *Journal*

DATE: _____

_____

_____

_____

_____

_____

_____

_____

_____

_____

_____

_____

_____

_____

CPSIA information can be obtained
at www.ICGtesting.com
Printed in the USA
LVHW060631291019
635550LV00005B/637/P